BTS

RISE OF BANGTAN

CARA J. STEVENS

HARPER

An Imprint of HarperCollinsPublishers

BTS: Rise of Bangtan

www.harpercollinschildrens.com

ISBN 978-0-06-288648-4

Production management: Stonesong Press, LLC
        Photo research: Heather Kemp
        Text and research: Cara Stevens
        Typography and design by studio2pt0

Photo Credits:
pp. ii: Kim Hee-Chul/EPA-EFE/Shutterstock; *2:* Matt Sayles/Invision/AP Images; *3:* Chelsea Lauren/Shutterstock; *4:* Imaginechina via AP Images; *7:* Ahn Young-Joon/AP Images; *8–9:* Ahn Young-Joon/AP/Shutterstock; *11:* Matt Sayles/Invision/AP Images; *15:* Michael Tran/FilmMagic/Getty Images; *16:* RB/Bauer-Griffin/GC Images/Getty Images; *19:* Ahn Young-Joon/AP/Shutterstock; *21:* Kim Hee-Chul/POOL/EPA-EFE/Shutterstock; *23:* Jordan Strauss/Invision/AP Images; *25:* bl Hubert Boesi/picture-alliance/dpa/AP Images; *27:* tl Lee-Young-Ho/Sipa via AP Images; *31:* t Sthanlee Mirador/Sipa via AP Images; *33:* br Imaginechina via AP Images; *35:* bl Invision/AP/Shutterstock; *38:* Kim Hee-Chul/EPA-EFE/Shutterstock; *39:* Jordan Strauss/Invision/AP Images; *43:* Chris Polk/AMA2017/Getty Images for dcp; *45:* ilgan Sports/Multi-Bits via Getty Images; *47:* RB/Bauer-Griffin/GC Images/Getty Images; *48:* Boontoom Sae-Kor/Shutterstock; *49:* Robyn Beck/AFP/Getty Images; *50:* Mark Ralston/AFP/Getty Images; *53:* Boontoom Sae-Kor/Shutterstock; *57:* Chelsea Lauren/Shutterstock; *61:* Chris Polk/AMA2017/Getty Images for dcp; *62:* Ahn Young-Joon/AP Images; *65:* Jeff Kravitz/AMA2017/Film Magic for dcp; *66:* Imaginechina via AP Images; *69:* C. Brandon/Redferns/Getty Images; *73:* Matt Sayles/Invision/AP images; *76:* Imaginechina via AP Images; *85:* Santiago Felipe/Getty Images; *88–89:* Michael Tran/FilmMagic/Getty Images; *91, 92:* Imaginechina via AP Images; *94:* Lee Young-Ho/SIPA USA via AP Images.

18 19 20 21 22 PC/LSCC 10 9 8 7 6

❖

First Edition

CONTENTS

JIN

Yonhap News/YNA/Newscom

RM

Yonhap News/YNA/Newscom

JIMIN

Yonhap News/YNA/Newscom

J-HOPE

Yonhap News/YNA/Newscom

SUGA

Yonhap News/YNA/Newscom

V

Yonhap News/YNA/Newscom

JUNGKOOK

Yonhap News/YNA/Newscom

INTRODUCTION

A K-pop boy band with a hip-hop influence, BTS's catchy songs, smooth moves, and adorable personalities have skyrocketed the seven members to worldwide idol status, earning them a top spot on charts around the globe. They even landed a place in *Guinness World Records* for having more Twitter engagement than any other musical group in the world in 2018.

Rebellious and edgy, romantic and sensitive, 90 percent of BTS's songs are written by the seven members of the group. Their hopes, dreams, fears, struggles, excitement, and passions are reflected in their songs, prompting an entire generation across the globe to join the BTS ARMY.

BTS debuted in 2013 with their breakout single "No More Dream." Their music is a mash-up of Western and Korean styles and includes star-studded collaborations with rappers and EDM stars such as Steve Aoki, the Chainsmokers, and Supreme Boi.

BTS GOES BY MANY DIFFERENT NAMES:
Bangtan Boys
Beyond the Scene
Bulletproof Boy Scouts
Bangtan Sonyeondan (방탄소년단) in Korean
Bōdan Shōnendan (防弾少年団) in Japanese

Who is BTS?

- Jin: vocalist, visual, hyung
- RM: rapper, producer, leader
- Suga: rapper, producer, group dad
- J-Hope: rapper, dancer, aegyo
- Jimin: dancer, vocalist, chocolate abs
- V: vocalist, visual, 4D
- Jungkook: dancer, vocalist, maknae

The boys' playful, casual energy offstage can seem surprising to fans whose first exposure to the group is their emotional, hard-edged lyrics and tight dancing style.

BULLETPROOF BOY SCOUTS: THE STORY BEHIND THE NAME

The group went through a few possible names before coming up with BTS, like Big Kids (because their management company is "Big Hit") and Young Nation. The name Bangtan translates to "bulletproof," a symbol of their goal to block out the world's bullets, standing tall and fighting for their beliefs no matter what kind of shade anyone throws at them. Sonyeondan translates to a group of boys or boy scouts.

"The meaning of 'bangtan' is to guard against something. So [our name] means that we will boldly defend our music and our value/worth."

—J-Hope

The acronym BTS has evolved since the group's debut, and the boys have expanded the meaning to Beyond the Scene in a nod to their connection with their fan base, ARMY.

THE LOGO

The band's open-door logo represents young people who aren't content with settling for their current reality, and are willing to open doors and go forward to achieve growth.

ARMY

An acronym for Adorable Representative MC for Youth, describing the army of fans devoted to spreading BTS's music and message of love, acceptance, and fun.

TIMELINE

2010–11 Big Hit Entertainment holds auditions for the group that becomes BTS

December 17, 2012 BTS Twitter account launches

June 9, 2013 Member lineup officially announced

June 11, 2013 "No More Dream" music video released

June 12, 2013 First album, 2 Cool 4 Skool, released

September 2, 2013 BTS's Rookie King variety show debuts

January 1, 2014 "Rookie of the Year" Golden Disc Award

February 12, 2014 "Boy In Luv" releases; that day it peaks at number three on the Billboard World Albums chart

March 29, 2014 BTS performs in front of three thousand fans at Global Official Fanclub ARMY First Muster concert in Seoul, South Korea

April 24, 2014 Makes Japanese debut with Wake Up

July 1–14, 2014 Stars in their first TV show, set in Los Angeles: American Hustle Life

September 9, 2014 Launches Hip Hop Monster webtoon series

January 23, 2015 Wins New Artist of the Year at Seoul Music Awards

February 10–19, 2015 First Japanese tour, "Wake Up: Open Your Eyes"

October 26, 2015 Becomes brand ambassadors for Puma

December 2, 2015 Wins Mnet Asian Music Award for Best World Performer

February 17, 2016 Wins Gaon Chart K-Pop Awards' World K-Pop Star Award

FAST FACT:

In 2017, "DNA" was the first K-pop group music video to reach two hundred million views on YouTube.

2016 Wings *hits number twenty-six on the Billboard 200–the highest K-pop album debut until 2018*

October 9, **2016** *"Blood Sweat & Tears" achieves all-kill, at number one on all eight Korean music charts: Melon, Mnet, Bugs, Olleh, Soribada, Genie, Naver, and Monkey3*

November 19, **2016** *Wins Melon Music Awards' Daesang, Best Album of the Year*

May 21, **2017** *Wins Billboard Music Awards' Top Social Artist Award, dethroning Justin Bieber, who had previously held the spot for six years running*

November 1, **2017** *Partners with Unicef to sponsor #ENDviolence and launches Love Myself*

July 31, **2017** *Wins Artist Award at the forty-fourth Korean Broadcasting Awards*

September 5, **2017** *Reaches eight million Twitter followers*

September 16, **2017** *Hits six million followers on their V Live channel*

September 18, **2017** *"DNA" becomes the first K-pop group single to hit the US iTunes top ten at number four*

September 18, **2017** *In its first twenty-four hours online, the "DNA" music video becomes eleventh most viewed video of all time*

September 22, **2017** *Hits the European charts in Sweden, Ireland, Italy, and Germany as well as the UK*

September 25, 2017 Becomes the first K-pop group to hit the Billboard Hot 100 with "DNA" at number eighty-five

September 26, 2017 Love Yourself: Her *hits number one on the Billboard World Albums chart*

November 12, 2017 BTS becomes the first Korean artist to reach ten million followers on Twitter and reaches eleven million one month later

November 19, 2017 Becomes the first K-pop group to perform at the American Music Awards

December 2, 2017 Takes home four group awards, and Suga is awarded the Hot Trend Award at the Melon Music Awards

January 11, 2018 Love Yourself: Her *takes home the Bonsang and Daesang Golden Disc Awards and the Digital Bonsang for "Spring Day"*

BONSANG VERSUS DAESANG

The Bonsang is a main award given to ten to twelve different artists, while a Daesang goes to one grand-prize winner.

February 14, 2018 You'll Never Walk Alone *wins Album of the Year for the first quarter while* Love Yourself: Her *wins for third quarter*

February 25, 2018 BTS is awarded the Bonsang and Daesang Awards at the Seoul Music Awards

February 28, 2018 Is awarded the Musician of the Year honor at the Korean Music Awards

March 9, 2018 Wins a non-music-related award at the iF Design Awards for Brand Identity

March 11, 2018 BTS ARMY works round the clock to ensure BTS wins for Best Fan Army at the iHeartRadio Music Awards. BTS also wins for Best Boy Band.

FAST FACT:
Love Yourself: Her **sold more than 1.2 million copies worldwide in less than one month.**

March 24, **2018** Kids across the USA vote BTS the Favorite Global Music Star at the Nickelodeon USA Kids' Choice Awards

April 16, **2018** BTS hits another new height with a record-breaking six Soompi awards for Artist of the Year, Album of the Year, Song of the Year, Best Choreography ("DNA"), Fuse Music Video of the Year ("DNA"), and Best Collaboration. V also wins for Best Idol Actor.

April 27, **2018** Receives award for Outstanding Achievement in Music and the Hall of Stars Award, plus Best Fandom Worldwide at the Asian Awards

April 29, **2018** Named brand ambassadors for Coca-Cola at the 2018 Russia World Cup

May 18, **2018** Love Yourself: Tear released

June 2, **2018** Love Yourself: Tear becomes the first K-pop album to debut at number one on Billboard's Top 200 album chart

BTS: BEFORE THE SCENE

Bang Si-hyuk—the Man behind BTS

Bang Si-hyuk, known as Hitman Bang, is BTS's creator and producer, and the founder and CEO of Big Hit Entertainment. His vision was to create a new kind of K-pop group based on substance as well as style.

The K-pop world is known for its churn-and-burn treatment of performers—finding raw talent and molding it through rigorous training, major plastic surgeries, and complete image reconstruction. These idols come and go like bubblegum pop stars from the 1980s in the US, shining brightly for a moment before burning out and fading into obscurity.

Bang had a different vision in mind when he set out to form BTS. His vision of "bulletproof boy scouts" would take raw talent and build on the members' internal fire, motivation, and personalities, to create a group worth idolizing.

Hitman Bang

Bang Si-hyuk had had a great deal of success in the Korean music world as a lyricist, composer, producer, and record executive well before Bangtan Sonyeondan hit the scene. Early in his career, he had partnered with Park Jin-young, the founder of JYP Entertainment, composing and arranging music while Jin-young wrote the lyrics.

Bang earned the nickname "Hitman" in the 1990s, as he and his partner created hit after hit with the groups they worked with. He left the partnership in 2005 to form Big Hit Entertainment, a new kind of entertainment company that would be more nurturing to its artists, provide more personalized attention, and let the trainees' personalities and artistic style shine through—a big divergence from the success machines that churn out K-pop stars focused more on a perfectly crafted image than on a true identity. He selected the group members carefully, finding artists who had a deep and abiding internal motivation as well as raw talent.

The first iteration of the group was a rap duo that included RM (then called RapMon), but later evolved into a seven-person idol group, which caused some of the trainees to jump ship. The personnel changed a few times along the way, but the resulting lineup was the perfect mix of talent, drive, spirit, personality, and "worldwide handsome."

ROOTING FOR
THE UNDERDOGS

Big Hit Entertainment was small potatoes compared to the corporate giants that dominate Korean mainstream media. That meant that there were no big corporate sponsors or PR machines to push the Bulletproof Boy Scouts out onto the scene. Instead, the small production company with a big heart supported their trainees full-on on their road to becoming idols.

Hard-core fans of BTS's well-choreographed dance routines and easy, polished manner in front of the cameras may be surprised to find that their initial debut was far from smooth or professional.

Early criticism of the group was harsh. Critics felt the boys were portraying watered-down versions of American rap and hip-hop culture without truly knowing what they were paying homage to. And in a sense, they were right. For all of their immersion in the music and dancing, most of the boys had never been on a plane or outside of the country, not to mention experienced true American culture. Suga and RM also faced backlash from the underground rap world they used to be a part of. Their former colleagues accused them of selling out, and criticism from their peers hit these adolescents hard, just as they were beginning to find their places in the music world.

"The boys just came up from the countryside. I didn't expect they would become famous on a worldwide scale."
—Bang Si-hyuk on BTS and the future of K-pop

But instead of letting the criticism get them down, Hitman Bang packed the boys up and sent them to Los Angeles, California, to experience the true nature of American street culture and music. Mentored by icons in dance, rap, and American music, the boys received a crash course in culture. The two-week experience became a hit reality show, American Hustle Life. It was so popular that fans waited impatiently, messaging each other about what would happen next, eager for the weekly episodes of a series that began with earnest, wide-eyed wonder and ended with newfound comfort and confidence.

After that, the group quickly skyrocketed to success, surprising even Hitman Bang.

RM'S BTS JOURNEY

One of the best things about the group is how in sync they are with every aspect of their public lives–their dance moves, their singing, their rapping, and their off-camera personalities. Like a well-constructed engine, each member makes a unique contribution with no sense of power struggle or clash.

"Back in 2010, I was introduced to Mr. Bang [Bang Si-hyuk], our executive producer [and CEO of Big Hit Entertainment]. I was an underground rapper and only sixteen years old, a freshman at high school. Bang thought I had potential as a rapper and lyricist, and we went from there. Then Suga joined us. J-Hope was really popular as a dancer in his hometown. We were the first three! We debuted as a collaboration between the seven of us in June 2013. We came together with a common dream to write, dance, and produce music that reflects our musical backgrounds as well as our life values of acceptance, vulnerability, and being successful. The seven of us have pushed each other to be the best we can be for the last four years. It has made us as close as brothers."
—RM, from *Time* magazine interview, June 2017

K-POP LIFE

The world of K-pop stardom is unlike any other. Groups are formed by agencies that send out a casting call or discover members on the street. Once members are selected, they become trainees. Not all members make it through training, and there is often a lot of shifting as the agency builds a perfect combination of performers and personalities that work well together. The training period for K-pop stars can last more than two years, with some members kept in the dark about whether they've made the cut until their debut. While training, members are schooled on how to be a superstar in front of the camera at all times. Trainees get full financial support from the agency while they are in training. They live together in a dorm and often work fourteen-hour days, honing different aspects of their public personas and performance skills. BTS trainees were teamed up in different ways, evaluated every month on their performance and progress, and given extra help in areas where they were falling behind.

After their big debut, it's the idols' turn to pay back the agency's investment by working even harder, making appearances on radio, TV, stage, in sponsored promotions, and in person, and releasing videos and records one after the other. BTS goes even further than most idols, posting about their offstage life on social media. Bangtan Boys are never without a camera nearby, recording their antics with selcas* and goofy home movies and sharing them online.

* selcas = selfie in K-pop

BTS: Behind the Stars

It took three years for a changing slate of trainees to come together to form the tight group that burst on the scene in 2013. Here's how the group developed.

2010 Big Hit scouted RM (as Runch Randa) and Hun-cheol (Iron) when they were part of hip-hop group DaeNamHyup. They formed the original BTS as a duo.

2010 Auditions led to the addition of i11evn, Suga, and J-Hope.

2011 i11evn left.

2011 Kidoh joined.

2011 Jungkook was cast after his failed audition at Super Star K2 made the rounds of the production companies.

2011 V joined around the time of Jungkook, but was the last to be announced–at their debut in 2013.

2013 Jin was originally studying to be an actor when he was recruited, and Jimin joined through an audition.

2013 Iron and Supreme Boi left.

BEHIND THE SCENES

- Jin was discovered while walking down the street.
- Suga almost quit as a trainee.
- V and RM worked for three years as trainees.
- Jimin trained for the shortest amount of time.
- Supreme Boi started with the group but quit training and now works with BTS as a producer.
- Jin was the last member to join.
- Trainees Jimin, J-Hope, and Jungkook all were sent for extra dance lessons.

Yonhap News/YNA/Newscom

Fans new to the band often have trouble telling members apart. For J-Hope and Jin, the internet blew up across the US when fans saw their handsome faces for the first time on national TV. Not knowing their names, a call went out over social media with their descriptions–which stuck and became new nicknames!

- "The one with the red hair and gold jacket"
  –J-Hope from his appearance on Dick Clark's New Year's Rockin' Eve
- "The third one from the left"
  –Jin from his appearance at the 2017 Billboard Music Awards

The group members spend twenty-four hours a day, seven days a week together whether they are on tour, at rehearsals, in the studio, or kicking back at the dorms. They have developed a true friendship that shows in their chemistry. They have also developed many nicknames for each other!

- Suga calls Jungkook "Jeon Jungkookie" and calls RM "Joonie."
- Everyone calls RM "Pa-gwe-e shin," which means "god of destruction."
- V is known to the group as "tae-tae" or "buin," which means "wife."
- Jimin is known as "Jiminnie," but RM also nicknamed him "Mo-jji Sek-shi," or "Sexy Mochi," because his cheeks are chubby–like little squishy rice cakes–but he is still a sexy idol.

COMEBACKS
Constantly Reinventing Themselves

The BTS arc is all about comebacks or album series. Each series shows a different side of the group, from their schoolboy persona to hard-edged wild boys to soulful young men exploring their spiritual side. While many fans have a clear favorite, if you're truly ARMY, you see each release as an opportunity to explore a new side of this complex and amazingly talented group.

The BTS Timeline by Era

- BTS hit the scene with the school trilogy–2 Cool 4 Skool, O!RUL8,2?, and Skool Luv Affair.

- They entered their Dark and Wild phase next, with their hit singles "Danger" and "War of Hormone."

- The Most Beautiful Moment in Life, Part 1 and Part 2, and Young Forever, brought them international recognition for their music and the introduction of their cinematic music video series.

- Wings earned them their first number-one hit in Korea and an Artist of the Year award at the 2016 Mnet Asian Music Awards. The MVs delved deep into the questions of existence and the search for spiritual truth.

- You'll Never Walk Alone was a repackaged version of Wings, but still sold seven hundred thousand copies.

- Love Yourself: Her skyrocketed the group to international fame with "DNA" and "Mic Drop."

- Love Yourself: Tear, the May 2018 follow-up to Love Yourself: Her hit number one on Billboard on its debut–the first K-pop release ever to achive that status.

BTS was the first group to have three music videos top three hundred million views: "DNA," "Fire," and "Dope."

The Steve Aoki remix of "Mic Drop," featuring Desiigner, is one of two songs by BTS to be certified gold.

MEET THE MEMBERS OF BTS

JIN

"I'm Jin. Worldwide Handsome."

FULL NAME: Kim Seok-jin 김석진

VOCALIST / VISUAL

BORN: December 4, 1992
HEIGHT: 5' 10"
HOMETOWN: Gwacheon, Gyeonggi-do, South Korea
LANGUAGES: Korean, English, Japanese, some Mandarin Chinese
EDUCATION: Konkuk University, degree in art and acting
JOINED BTS: 2011

The oldest member, Jin is "the self-proclaimed 'big brother'" or hyung of the group, and jokes that he is also "in charge of having the amazingly handsome face."

Jin learned how to cook when he first joined the band and was put on a strict diet. He's the ultimate foodie and loves to prepare food, talk about food, tell stories about food, and of course eat! He is known for being a big joker, and even if his jokes aren't funny, when he laughs at his own jokes, it's infectious!

Even though Jin is the hyung of the group, he has an older brother at home. At the dorm, however, Jin really does act like the grown-up. He wakes up early and is in charge of the kitchen and cleaning the house.

EAT JIN!

In September 2014, Bangtan Bomb featured a video of Jin eating salad. To the casual observer, this was nothing special, but this moment actually marked the beginning of Jin's mukbang* career in his series *Eat Jin*. Over the course of about thirty videos, Jin eats in a cafeteria, in a hotel room, in the kitchen, with friends, and while talking with a manager off-camera. He eats a variety of foods and even prepares food on camera at times. The *Eat Jin* playlist can be found on BangtanTV's YouTube channel, with several bonus mukbang videos also on V Live.

* A mukbang is a video of a Korean idol enjoying large quantities of food on camera while talking to the audience.

JIN'S ADORABLE FLUFFY PALS

Jin had a puppy named Jjangu who passed away. He adopted two adorable little sugar gliders, which he, of course, named after his favorite foods–two different kinds of fish cake!

Sugar gliders are tiny exotic pets the size of a small hamster. They are very social and need a lot of attention, which Jin is happy to give them every day, even after a long day of practice. While five of the group's members have pets, only Jin's and V's pets live with the boys in the dorm.

Yonhap News/YNA/Newscom

Yonhap News/YNA/Newscom

FAST FACTS:

- Jin was a college student when he was discovered on the street and invited to audition for the group.

- Jin and Jimin are gym buddies. They often work out together. But at home, Jin chose Suga as his roommate.

- His ideal girl is sweet, domestic, and could be a good wife.

"Most of our music is about how we perceive the world and how we try to persist as normal, average human beings."

RM

FULL NAME: Kim Nam-joon 김남준
(aka Rap Monster, Runch Randa, RapMon, Namjoon)

LEADER / RAPPER / PRODUCER

BORN: September 12, 1994
HEIGHT: 5' 11"
HOMETOWN: Ilsan, Goyang, South Korea
LANGUAGES: Korean, English, Japanese
EDUCATION: Global Cyber University with honors in broadcasting and performing arts; studied in New Zealand
EARLY CAREER: Breakout in 2008 as Runch Randa
JOINED BTS: 2010 as first member

RUNCHI RANDA

RAPMON

RM is the leader of BTS, and is also the one who does most of the talking in BTS's English-language interviews. RM developed a passion for rap at a young age, and grew up watching videos of American rappers. He became an underground rapper and worked with popular artists before becoming the first member selected to join BTS.

RM is tough and edgy but not scary as his monster name suggests. Offstage, RM is playful and full of deep thoughts. He's the voice of the group when speaking English, as he speaks with barely a hint of an accent and knows all the colloquial slang.

While RM is a master rapper, his talents don't quite make it all the way down to his hands and feet. When he was a trainee, his dance teachers gave him the ironic nickname "Dance Prodigy" when he couldn't manage to get any of the moves right. Namjoon's group-mates report he is always breaking things at home, when they travel, and pretty much everywhere he goes, but his brilliant mind and caring personality make it all worthwhile.

RAP MONSTER

Yonhap News/YNA/Newscom

Yonhap News/YNA/Newscom

NAMJOON

Yonhap News/YNA/Newscom

Yonhap News/YNA/Newscom

Yonhap News/YNA/Newscom

FAST FACTS:

• RM taught himself English while watching the TV show *Friends*.

• His dog is named Rapmon.

• His ideal is a sexy, feminine woman he can have long conversations with.

"After we debuted, I went back to the dorm and sat there staring blankly. I could not believe it, that a kid from a poor Daegu family would be able to make it."

SUGA

FULL NAME: Min Yoon-gi 민윤기

RAPPER / PRODUCER

BORN: March 9, 1993
HEIGHT: 5' 8"
HOMETOWN: Buk-gu, Daegu, South Korea
EDUCATION: ApGuJeong High School
EARLY CAREER: Underground rapper named Gloss in D-Town
JOINED BTS: 2010, originally joined as a producer

Like RM, Suga was also an underground rapper before joining BTS. But his talents don't stop at busting a rhyme on the mic. Suga is also a master at songwriting, producing, and playing the piano. Suga is the second oldest of the group, after Jin. In 2016, Suga released a solo album under the name Agust D. In it, he revealed that he had been battling depression, OCD, and social anxiety from the time he left home to pursue his dream. Through therapy and with the help of his BTS-mates and the BTS ARMY, Suga was able to overcome these obstacles, and he expresses gratitude to his fans and the BTS community for their love and support.

FAST FACTS:
- Even though Suga's name sounds sweet, he doesn't have a sweet tooth at all and prefers light, savory foods.
- He had an appendectomy in 2013, which earned him the nickname Mr. Appendix.
- He is such a big fan of sleeping, he could easily earn the nickname "Nap Monster."
- Suga has strong likes and dislikes that really shape his personality. He enjoys sleeping, taking photos, playing basketball, and quiet places. He dislikes crowds and dancing.
- On camera and in the press, Suga and the rest of the group joke about his love for sleep.
- His ideal is someone who is smart, calm, and has a similar personality to him.

AGUST D MIXTAPE

Suga's solo artist name, Agust D, is "Suga" backward plus DT, which stands for Daegu Town, his childhood home.

The day after the Japanese release of "Forever Young," another showstopping surprise dropped onto the music scene: Suga's self-produced solo mixtape. Consisting of ten songs, the album starts out with a sample from a famous song by James Brown, then hits listeners with an introduction to Suga the artist and the rapper, as he sings, "This K-pop category ain't enough size for me."

Suga's songs have an edge to them when they're not softened by the aegyo poses and group choreography of BTS, and he is free to speak for himself through his alter ego, Agust D. Through each of the ten tracks, he tells the story of his past, his rise to fame, and his life as an idol.

Yonhap News/YNA/Newscom

Yonhap News/YNA/Newscom

Yonhap News/YNA/Newscom

"My name has the deepest meaning out of all the others in this group. [Laughs] You know how in Pandora's box after everything else left, the only thing remaining was hope, right? I put 'hope' in my name to be a hopeful existence in the group. I got the J from my last name, Jung. That's how I became J-Hope."

J-HOPE

FULL NAME: Jung Ho-seok 정호석

RAPPER / DANCER

BORN: February 18, 1994
HEIGHT: 5' 10"
HOMETOWN: Gwangju, South Korea
EARLY CAREER: He studied at a famous dance academy in Gwangju and had a contract with entertainment company JYP before he joined Big Hit. He was also a member of Neuron, a street dance crew.
JOINED BTS: 2010
NICKNAME: Hobi

J-Hope is a beagle with a bundle of energy onstage, showcasing his impressive dance skills, unique rapping style, and adorable aegyo expressions. Before joining BTS, J-Hope had already achieved some fame as a street dancer and competitor. He won a national dance competition in South Korea in 2008. Ho-seok, also known to friends and fans as Hobi, focused more on vocals than rap in the early days, which explains his smooth, singsong rapping technique. His positive attitude led him to choose his stage name as he aspired to be a source of hope and light for his fans.

Before he debuted with BTS, J-Hope belonged to a street dance crew called Neuron. "While promoting underground with my street dance team, I did a lot of popping. In popping, there's another sub-genre called Boogaloos, and that was the one I did the most. I got a lot of prizes and performed a lot while promoting."

FAST FACTS:

• J-Hope moved to Seoul in 2010.

• While J-Hope is known for his cute aegyo poses, he wasn't always a fan of making faces for the camera.

• In the MV for his solo song "Daydream," J-Hope offers a nod to the book *The Hitchhiker's Guide to the Galaxy* when he receives a message from the book's main character, Arthur, saying "Don't panic."

• His ideal match is a supportive girl who likes books and is a great cook.

Yonhap News/YNA/Newscom

Yonhap News/YNA/Newscom

"Names like Baby J and Kid were some options, but I decided that Jimin was the best and ended up using my real name."

JIMIN

FULL NAME: Park Ji-min 박지민

DANCER / VOCALIST

BORN: October 13, 1995
HEIGHT: 5' 8"
HOMETOWN: Busan, South Korea
EDUCATION: Busan High School, then transferred to Korea Arts High School and completed his coursework at Global Cyber University
JOINED BTS: 2012

Before auditioning for BTS, Jimin was a modern dance student at an arts-focused high school, along with fellow band member V. He is a perfectionist when it comes to just about anything, but he also has a soft, caring personality underneath it all. Jimin's fellow BTS members make fun of him for being short, but he takes it in stride.

Jimin moved into the dormitory in May 2012, a year after V. Jungkook was living there at the time as well. Dorm life wasn't the only new experience for Jiminnie. He was the new kid at school as well. V took him under his wing, introduced him to his friends, and they ate together every day, getting ramen and snacks from the school cafeteria.

When he is on camera, the focus is usually on Jimin's smooth moves and chocolate abs, but his soft singing voice can be heard in his solo track "Lie," which he also wrote himself. The song is about insecurities, self-doubt, and the pressure he puts on himself to always say and do the right thing.

Onstage and off, Jimin supports his fellow group members wholeheartedly and is always worried about letting them down. He has been known to take single-minded dedication to practice and fitness too far, like the time he got a nosebleed during practice from working too hard.

AWARDS

Melon Music Award : New Artist of the Year (2013)
Golden Disc Award: Newcomer Award (2014)
Melon Music Award: Best Male Dance Award (2015)
Golden Disc Award: Disc Bonsang (2016)

Yonhap News/YNA/Newscom

Yonhap News/YNA/Newscom

FAST FACTS:

• Jimin used to battle weight issues, and claims he ate six meals a day when he and V were in high school. As an idol, Jimin follows a strict diet and exercise routine and takes pride in his rock-hard "chocolate" abs. When the group is on tour, Jimin feels like his six-pack gets a little soft, but he gets right back on track when they return home, exercising every day with Jungkook to stay in shape.

• Jimin's ideal girl will definitely have a nice personality.

> "Although people usually think what I say is funny,
> I don't do it purposefully to please others."

V

FULL NAME: Kim Tae-hyung 김태형

VOCALIST

BORN: December 30, 1995
HEIGHT: 5' 10"
HOMETOWN: Born in Daegu, South Korea, and grew up in Geochang
LANGUAGES: Korean, fluent Japanese
EDUCATION: Korea Art School and Global Cyber University
EARLY CAREER: Acted in the Korean drama *Hwarang*
JOINED BTS: 2011

V embraces all kinds of creative endeavors, not just music. He's a big fan of art, and he also acted in the Korean drama *Hwarang*, playing the character Hansung from 2016 to 2017. Some fans refer to him as the 4D member–a K-pop term for someone who is offbeat, quirky, and a little out-of-this-world. He tries to speak English with an American accent sometimes, which many fans think is simply "adorkable"!

V received serious shade from fans and haters after he grabbed the microphone and sang the song "Loser," by Big Bang, during the acceptance speech at *M! Countdown* when BTS beat the group EXID. V and his supporters insist that he meant no harm with his choice of song, as he is simply a hard-core Big Bang fan. Later, in an apologetic tweet, V tweeted that he listened to "I Need U," "Bae Bae," and "Loser" every day and that he had meant no harm by his choice of song.

Yonhap News/YNA/Newscom

Yonhap News/YNA/Newscom

FAST FACTS:

- Tae-hyung hails from farm country. He is the oldest of three siblings, with a younger sister and a younger brother.

- V stands for *victory*–his hope for success for BTS–but it wasn't the only option for Tae-hyung's stage name. He had also considered Six and Lex before settling on V.

- V has a soft spot for fluffy animals. He has three dogs who live with his family–Soonshin, Ssyongssyong, and a Pomeranian puppy named Yeontan–plus a cat named Kkanji.

- V played the saxophone for three years when he was younger because his father told him that all singers should also know how to play an instrument.

- He loves anything unique and different, and in his spare time can be found looking up obscure music on the internet.

- He loves amusement parks and wild rides, although he hates scary things like ghosts.

- His nicknames are Tae-tae (which is easier to say than Tae-hyung) and Blank Tae (because he often has a blank stare when he's dancing).

- V has a very specific idea of his ideal girl. She should be frugal with her spending and will get on his case if he spends too much. She would also consider buying a car before she bought a house, she would make good hot chocolate, and she would be loyal and generous with her parents.

"A lot of things have changed because I went to America. When I was a trainee it was like I was told to practice dance, but it was completely different in America. It was really free."

JUNGKOOK

FULL NAME: Jeon Jeong-guk 전정국

DANCER / VOCALIST

BORN: September 1, 1997
HEIGHT: 5' 10"
HOMETOWN: Busan, South Korea
EDUCATION: Seoul School of Performing Arts
EARLY CAREER: Seoul School of Performing Arts
JOINED BTS: 2011
NICKNAMES: Kookie, Golden Maknae

Jungkook is the maknae (youngest) of the group and is also referred to as Golden Maknae because he's good at singing, dancing, rapping, and sports. Although he often takes lead vocals, he is the quietest member offstage. Before he was old enough to start high school, Jungkook auditioned for South Korean talent show *Superstar K* and was an instant hit. He signed with Big Hit Entertainment, and joined BTS when he was fifteen. While training to become a global superstar, he also received formal instruction from the Seoul School for the Performing Arts, graduating a year late in 2017.

Jungkook is well-known for his singing and dancing skills, but he's also a great overall athlete, whether racing, arm wrestling, doing archery, or even bowling. He is also a talented artist—it runs in his family.

Jungkook may be the youngest member, but his many talents make him quite the Korean Renaissance man. He is not only a talented singer in Korean, he sings just as well in English, Japanese, Chinese, and Vietnamese, both with accompaniment or a cappella. As fans know, he's also an amazing dancer.

But that's not all. Jungkook has many other talents, and his group-mates are quick to share stories and praise any time they get in front of the camera.

FAST FACTS:

- In his spare time, Jungkook loves gaming, whether on his phone, playing console games, or in an arcade. He is a big fan of the game Overwatch. When he's not playing games, he likes to read books and comics.

- He can speak decent Japanese and English.

- His favorite subject in school was gym class.

- He has an older brother named Jung Hyun.

- Jungkook once sent a video to audition for a Korean singing show. When his tape went viral within the industry, this Golden Maknae became the most in-demand trainee in South Korea!

- His ideal is someone who is about five foot two, is smart, has nice skin, and is good at singing.

QUIZ: HOW WELL
DO YOU KNOW BTS?

Think you know everything there is to know about these idols? Use the key to put the right BTS member's letter by their answer, then check your answers below. Give yourself one point for each correct answer.

A - Jin
B - RM
C - Suga
D - V
E - J-Hope
F - Jimin
G - Jungkook

1. FAVORITE FOOD

Fish
Kimchi
Ramen and fried chicken
Sweets
Spicy food
Fruit
Meat, meat, and more meat

2. PERSONALITY

Smart
4D
Leader
Lazy
Playful / Aegyo
Competitive
Supportive

3. ROLE IN THE HOUSE

Grandfather
Making a mess
Teasing
Laundry
Sleeping
Doing his own thing
Being supportive

4. FAVORITE MOVIE

Inception
The Matrix
Southpaw
Always
Eternal Sunshine of the Spotless Mind
Iron Man
About Time

5. THE PETS OF BTS

Three dogs and one cat
Sugar gliders Eomuk and Odeng
A dog named Holly
A dog named Mickey
A dog named Gureum (or Cloudie)

6. ROLE MODEL

Kanye West
T.O.P. from Big Bang
Lil Wayne
G-Dragon from Big Bang
Beenzino
Eric Bannet
Taeyang from Big Bang

7. FAVORITE COLOR

Pink
White
Green
Gray
Blue / black
Black, pink, and purple
Black

8. NEVER LEAVE HOME WITHOUT

Water
ChapStick
Pillow
Camera

9. NAME MEANING

The genius from the south
Be a great treasure
A glowing pearl
Fame
Be the nation's pillar
Wisdom reaching to the skies
Hope in the face of adversity

10. WHAT HE THINKS DEFINES A MASCULINE MAN

Strength / knowledge
Presence
Confidence
Responsibility
Face
Taking care of others
Manners and passion

YOUR SCORE: ___ /65

TRAINEE DAYS

From Trainees to Idols–the Beginning of a K-Pop Phenomenon

Holding auditions and training a pop group together for several months or even years before they debut is standard procedure in the K-pop industry. Groups live together in dorms, where they eat, sleep, rehearse, and hang out together 24/7.

When Bang held auditions for group members, he didn't just focus on the music or dancing. Each of his chosen trainees was self-motivated and passionate about the work from an early age. Bang's philosophy is that while he could teach them to sing, dance, pose, look, and act like superstars, they all needed to come to the training with a love of music and a passion for the work.

While a number of bigger Korean pop entertainment firms have gotten a bad reputation for mistreating their trainees and their stars, Big Hit Entertainment has a different approach. Label boss Bang Si-hyuk gives trainees and idols like the Bangtan Boys more independence in exchange for completely candid and often harsh but fair criticism.

FAST FACT:
When "No More Dream" was released, Jin was twenty-one and Jungkook was only sixteen!

"People think we have an exaggerated life since we're singers, but I actually just sleep, play on my phone . . . that's all. There's nothing else to do in the dorms besides sleep."
—RM in group interview with *AJ x The Star*

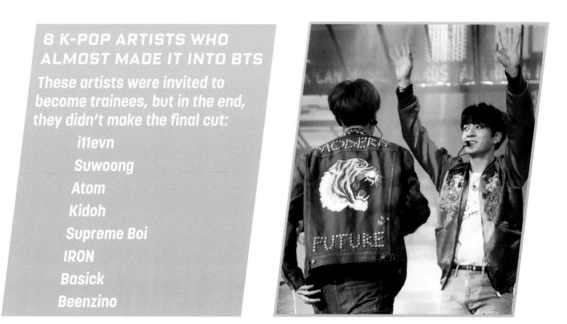

8 K-POP ARTISTS WHO ALMOST MADE IT INTO BTS

These artists were invited to become trainees, but in the end, they didn't make the final cut:

- **i11evn**
- **Suwoong**
- **Atom**
- **Kidoh**
- **Supreme Boi**
- **IRON**
- **Basick**
- **Beenzino**

Life at Home

When the group first formed, all seven idols shared one room.

As they moved up the ladder of success, they paired up into doubles. They played rock, paper, scissors to decide who would get the single room. The Golden Maknae, Jungkookie, won, even though he is the youngest.

In 2018, the idols moved into a big new trainee dorm with six bedrooms. J-Hope and Jimin are the only two members to share a room, and they say they wouldn't have it any other way.

IDOL NIGHTS

"If you asked most Americans to name just one Korean performing artist in the last year, odds are high the answer would have been BTS. Bangtan Sonyeondan's music has taken over the world in recent years, and 2017 was the year they finally cracked the notoriously competitive US market. The seven-member Korean boy band performed at the American Music Awards in November, the first K-pop act to do the honors. They've also appeared on *Ellen* and *Jimmy Kimmel*, leaving a trail of online hysteria and viral clips in their wake from a devout—and constantly growing—fanbase."

—*Forbes* magazine, March 27, 2018

BTS on Tour

- March 29, **2014** Global Official Fanclub ARMY First Muster, Seoul, South Korea (3,000 fans)

- July 14, **2014** Show & Prove Concert, Los Angeles, California (250 fans)

- October 17, **2014**–August 29, **2015** BTS Live Trilogy Episode II: The Red Bullet, South Korea, Japan, Philippines, Singapore, Thailand, Taiwan, Malaysia, Australia, USA, Mexico, Brazil, Chile, Hong Kong

- February 10-19, **2015** BTS First Japan Tour, Wake Up: Open Your Eyes, Japan

- March 28-29, **2015** BTS Live Trilogy Episode I: BTS Begins, South Korea (6,500 fans)

- November 27, **2015**–March 23, **2016** BTS Live The Most Beautiful Moment in Life on Stage, South Korea, Japan

- January 24, **2016** BTS Second Muster [ZIP CODE : 22920], South Korea (9,000 fans)

- November 12-13, **2016** BTS Third Muster [ARMY.ZIP +], South Korea (38,000 fans)

- May 7-August 14, **2016** BTS Live The Most Beautiful Moment in Life on Stage: Epilogue, South Korea, Taiwan, Macau, China, Japan, Philippines, Thailand

- February 18-December 10, **2017** BTS Live Trilogy Episode III (Final Chapter): The Wings Tour, North America, South America, Asia, Australia

- January 13-14, **2018** BTS Fourth Muster [Happy Ever After]. Seoul, South Korea (40,000 fans)

ARE YOU ARMY?
@BTS_TWT

All About BTS ARMY

The BTS ARMY is the driving force behind the group's meteoric rise to popularity. While they sing and conduct interviews almost exclusively in Korean (with a few English and Japanese phrases thrown in every now and then), the group has worldwide appeal largely thanks to the ARMY of fans who translate lyrics and interviews, fuel campaigns to boost sales and social media chatter, and spread the news far and wide across the internet in many languages.

BTS members recognize the importance of their fan base, thanking their ARMY for every rousing online fan-driven success.

Joining the Official BTS ARMY

ARMY memberships are only open occasionally. The best way to stay on top of an application window is on their official Facebook page.

To become a member, you first need to be a member of their fancafe on daum.net, as well as a registered member of the e-commerce site Interpark, www.globalinterpark.com. Both are free to join.

BTS was the first K-pop group to earn its own Twitter emoji. The emoji mirrors their bulletproof vest logo. In a Twitter-wide search for their biggest fan bases, ARMY all over the world used the emoji to compete, and in the end, Brazilian, Turkish, and Russian ARMYs won for using the hashtag the most during the competition.

Becoming Unofficially ARMY (but Still Awesome)

It's a challenge to join the official group, and there's less benefit to joining if you live outside of South Korea, where most of the fan benefits are based, but that shouldn't stop you from becoming an adorable representative yourself.

The fan site usbtsarmy.com has up-to-date news, info, and tutorials on joining the official army fanclub and fancafe in English.

Fanclub, Fancafe—What's the Difference?

In Korean fandom, there are two ways to support your bias (favorite idol or group), fanclubs and fancafes. A fancafe is free to join, while a fanclub requires paid membership.

BTS Fancafe: http://cafe.daum.net/bangtan

The fancafe is free to join; however, the site is entirely in Korean, making it difficult to sign up and almost impossible to follow if you don't speak or read Korean, even if you have a good web-translating program. Fancafe membership lets you chat live with other ARMY members, ask questions directly to Big Hit and BTS, get official updates on fansigns, recordings, and news, leave messages for your favorite idols, and access messages from the members themselves . . . Yes, they actually DO check their fancafe messages—especially J-Hope, who loves checking in on the fancafe in his spare time. They often post selcas so you can get your daily dose of awesome even if you can't read the captions.

The fancafe is hosted on the major Korean web portal Daum.

Fanclub Benefits

Membership in the official BTS ARMY entitles you to different benefits each year. The recruitment window opens in spring and lasts for only a couple of weeks, with announcements on the official BTS social media outlets like Twitter, Instagram, and on their official page.

Fan Chants

K-pop fans are ardent supporters of their idols. This is especially evident at concerts, where fans actively show their support for the group by learning the chant and reciting it in unison. Audience participation comes in the form of specific lyrics in Korean or English or simply recitations of the group members' given names in a specific order:

"Kim Nam-joon! Kim Seok-jin! Min Yoon-gi! Jung Ho-seok! Park Ji-min! Kim Tae-hyung! Jeon Jeong-guk! BTS!"
–The basic BTS fan chant

The effect amps up the idols on stage and the audience, too.

"BTS fans—the 'ARMY'—tell us about their feelings, failures, passions and struggles all the time. We are often inspired by [them], because we try to write about how real young people—like the seven of us—face real-life issues. So our fans inspire us and give us a direction to go as musicians. And of course, their love and support keeps us going."
—RM, *Time* magazine interview

UNOFFICIAL FAN BASES

The Amino Army is an online community of fans across the globe who are dedicated to sharing their love and knowledge of the band and their members. It's free to join and you can access it on the web at https://aminoapps.com/c/Btsarmy/ or through the Amino app. The Amino Army features blog posts, quizzes, polls, fan art, memes, and more covering all aspects of the group, the music, and the seven artists who make it all possible.

BTS Diary is another source for all things BTS. It's updated several times a day with breaking news, countdowns to new releases, and translations of interviews from international magazines and news sources.

BTS Wiki is a crowdsourced wiki that allows anyone to contribute to a growing body of information on all things BTS. You can access the wiki and contribute to its growth at http://the-bangtan-boys.wikia.com/wiki/BTS_Wiki.

Conventions are super popular with BTS fans, too. Hundreds got together at KCON, the Korean Culture Convention in Los Angeles, when the seven appeared there in 2014.

FAST FACT:
Follow the hashtag #RMusic for RM's personal music recommendations on Twitter.

Official Sites

- BTS Official Site bts.ibighit.com
- BTS Shop btsofficialshop.com
- BTS Shop (English version) en.btsofficialshop.com
- BTS Blog btsblog.ibighit.com
- BTS V Live channels.vlive.tv/FE619/video
- BTS Weibo weibo.com/BTSbighit
- BTS Fancafe cafe.daum.net/BANGTAN
- BTS Japan Official Fanclub https://bts-official.jp
- Soundcloud https://soundcloud.com/bangtan

Forum

- BangtanBase–a forum dedicated to BTS https://bangtanbase.com

SPOTIFY

BTS members each have their own playlist with each member holding up a letter. When shown in order, they spell out MICDROP.

Jungkook: I Am Listening to It Right Now by BTS

Jin's GA CHI DEUL EUL LAE? by BTS

Jimin's JOAH? JOAH! by BTS

SUGA's Hip-Hop Replay by BTS

RM's Heavy Rotations by BTS

J-Hope's JAM by BTS

V's Join Me by BTS

ARMY FRIENDS ARE HERE TO HELP

Spreading Love and Positivity, ARMY Gives Back

The Army Help Centre, www.spreadlovepositivity.org, is a team of BTS fans from around the world who volunteer their time to help BTS fans young and old when they need emotional help or support. AHC counselors are volunteer psychologists and psychology students who provide help in more than thirty different languages, round the clock, online and over social media.

For those who want someone to talk to who will listen and understand them without judgment, AHC can be contacted via DM on Twitter. Although they are not professionals, they will be happy to share about how to deal with certain situations, like problems in school, being bullied, or social anxiety, and can direct you on how to get professional help if you need it.

The center has received around three thousand DMs and counting since @BTS_AHC was created!

They can also be reached via email at slp@spreadlovepositivity.org or btsarmyhelpcentre@gmail.com, and they will connect people with a counselor to communicate with directly.

AHC and Spread Love Positivity are not affiliated with BTS or Big Hit Entertainment.

"I have found a family in this fandom that have become a valuable part of my daily life. I care about each and every ARMY. We are a family and nothing can touch us if we stay united and take care of one another. I love my family."
—Valfroy Aissatou, founder of AHC

DISCOGRAPHY

2 Cool 4 Skool (CD, Album)	2013
0!RUL8,2? (CD, Mini, MiniAlbum)	2013
Wake Up	2014
Skool Luv Affair	2014
Dark & Wild (CD)	2014
The Most Beautiful Moment in Life, Part 1	2015
The Most Beautiful Moment in Life Part 2	2015
Dark & Wild (CD, Album + DVD-V)*	2015
花樣年華 Pt.1 (CD + DVD-V)*	2015
Skool Luv Affair (Album+DVD) (CD + DVD)	2015
화양연화 Young Forever	2016
Wings 'W'	2016
Youth*	2016
You Never Walk Alone	2017
Kayonenka Young Forever (2xCD, Album + DVD-V)	2017
Love Yourself: Her (CD, Album, EP)	2017
Face Yourself**	2018
Love Yourself: Tear	2018

Korean releases by Big Hit Entertainment
* Japanese releases by Pony Canyon
** Universal Music, Def Jam Recordings, Virgin Music

Digital downloads are super convenient, but did you know that some of the physical albums contain hidden bonus tracks?

2 Cool 4 Skool
- Path
- Skit: On the Start Line

Love Yourself: Her
- Ocean/Sea
- Skit: Hesitation and Fear

In May 2018, Love Yourself: Tear, sung mainly in Korean, became the first primarily foreign-language No. 1 Billlboard album in more than twelve years.

Stars Join In
The Bangtan Boys' mad K-pop skills got a little help from celebrefans. A few collaborations to note:

When BTS met up with Andrew Taggart from the Chainsmokers at the Billboard Music Awards, the result was the collaboration "Best of Me" on Love Yourself: Her.

BTS's "Mic Drop (remix)" with Steve Aoki went Gold in the US and spent ten weeks on the Billboard Hot 100.

Not only do the Bangtan Boys rap, sing, and dance like true idols, they are also stellar songwriters. RM, Suga, J-Hope, and Jungkook also have producing credits to their names.

"The members teased me when I first attempted writing lyrics. I think it is necessary for producers to know how to sing, rap, and compose. A song will be more meaningful if I construct the song from start to finish, instead of using a beat made by someone else."

—RM

FAST FACT:
Love Yourself: Her preorder sales reached 1.05 million copies.

THE MEANING BEHIND
THE MUSIC

Brainier Than the Average Pop Group

There is an intellectual subtext to BTS MVs that is clear even if you don't understand the words. The most notably deep video is the short film "Wings." RM opens the video with a speech in English: "The realms of day and night. Two different worlds coming from two opposite poles mingled during this time." It is a line taken from a classic German novel, *Demian*, by Hermann Hesse, written in 1919. The novel explores the struggle between the world of illusion and the real world of spiritual truth; the superficial world of what we show others and the true nature of who we are. Pretty deep for a bunch of hoobaes (novices).

Music with a Message

As RM explained in an interview on KBS, the Korean Broadcasting Network, the group likes to include literary references in their songs to expand the connection people make to the messages.

The Bangtan Boys' songs revolve around everyday teen struggles like love and school, but don't shy away from the heavier-hitting issues of societal norms, sexuality, and mental illness.

FAST FACT:

A Künstlerroman is a work that describes an artist's coming-of-age story. *Demian* is a classic example. Most of BTS's songs and MVs can be considered Künstlerroman works, too.

"Our BTS team identity consists of fighting off prejudices and oppression and protecting the integrity of music. We try to connect those messages together. We are striving to communicate that through music."

—J-Hope, KBS interview

INSPIRING READS

They can rap. They can dance. They are handsome. And they are well-read, too. Youth across the globe have since discovered Demian, the classic German novel Namjoon was seen carrying and reading in various photos and videos, and now ARMY are paying attention to other books the boys are reading, too. Put these on your reading list to gain a deeper appreciation for your favorite BTS tracks.

Life Lessons, *Elisabeth Kübler-Ross (Suga)*

About Her, *Banana Yoshimoto (Suga)*

Kitchen, *Banana Yoshimoto (RM)*

Demian, *Hermann Hesse (RM)*

Twenty Thousand Leagues Under the Sea *and*
Around the World in 80 Days, *Jules Verne (J-Hope)*

Lord Chesterfield's Letters, *Phillip Chesterfield (V)*

IQ84, Kafka on the Shore, *and* Norwegian Wood, *Haruki Murakami (RM)*

Me Before You, *Jojo Moyes (RM)*

The Stranger, *Albert Camus (RM)*

The Catcher in the Rye, *J. D. Salinger (RM)*

The Hitchhiker's Guide to the Galaxy, *Douglas Adams (RM)*

"As BTS, we, as a team, always try to highlight stories of growing up and of people in their teens and twenties. That's our main message."

—RM, KBS interview

THE MOVES

As trainees, the boys practiced around ten hours a day, with some members even getting up in the middle of the night to rehearse for fear of letting the others down in practice the next day. Performance director and choreographer Son Seong Deuk has cut rehearsal time down to four hours per day as he feels the members have gained a more intuitive feel for what they have down and how they can make their performances even tighter.

- J-Hope leads the charge, combining his smooth hip-hop and freestyle moves with his masterful popping and isolation.

- Jimin trained as a contemporary dancer, with clean lines and a fluid dance style. He moves like water onstage.

- Jungkook trained in tae kwon do, which gives his dancing grace, power, and energy.

These three do the heavy lifting for RM, V, Jin, and Suga, who didn't have any dance background before they became trainees.

If you're inspired by their moves, you can follow along with YouTubers who have slowed down the videos and broken down each move step by step. Some vloggers offer mirrored steps so you can recreate the moves exactly as the dancers perform them, while others show you how to do the moves as you see them on-screen and on stage.

BTS: BREAKING
THE SCREEN

In their spare time when they're not singing, rapping, dancing, composing, performing, recording, rehearsing, eating, vlogging, meeting fans, making MVs, or competing on game shows, they've also created their own webtoon, emoji, and game app.

Is there anything these bulletproof boy scouts can't do?

FAST FACT:
Webtoons (web+[car]toon) are digital manga or comics that
scroll down in a continuous vertical layout.

Hip Hop Monster

Seven members, seven aegyo characters who bear an uncanny resemblance to them: Big Hit developed characters in collaboration with entertainment company CJ E&M based on the members' personalities, appearance, and hobbies. They were revealed in the BTS online Meet & Greet fan meeting in 2014, and became the now iconic line of dolls, stickers, characters, and Hip Hop Monster webtoon.

The comic takes place in a school, where the seven characters form a club and have minor adventures. There were forty-four episodes created in all. The English translations can be found on the BTS Diary site under the Webtoons menu: https://btsdiary.com/hip-hop-monster.

We On: Be the Shield

Their next webtoon series has a completely different manga-style look and feel. It is based on the song of the same name from their album O!RUL8,2? The story follows the seven characters (who have the same names but not the same personalities as the group's members) protecting Earth from invading monsters with their superpowers. The story unfolds in twenty-nine chapters and has only had one season. The English translations can be found on the BTS Diary website in the Webtoons menu as well at https://btsdiary.com/picture/webtoon/we-on-be-the-shield.

BT21: The Cuteness Invasion Friends Creators

In a collaboration between Line Friends and BTS, the boys created their own characters and Line Friends brought them to life in the form of cushions, plushies, fashion and accessories, and characters with a load of personality. In true BTS style, the whole development process was caught on camera. You can see the story and meet the characters at the official site, www.bt21.com, and purchase official merchandise on Amazon.com (search for BT21).

Puzzle Star

BT21 the Game is a swipe-and-blast game featuring the cute characters the boys created with Line Friends. You can download the game and the emoji characters for free on Google Play or the App Store.

BTS ON TV

There are almost daily free BTS updates on VLive.TV and the BangtanTV YouTube channel, with additional premium content available by subscription on V Live and YouTube Red. A big daily dose of these K-pop idols!

VLIVE.TV

V Live is an online broadcaster that lets celebrities like BTS connect directly with fans. The BTS channel features several series including Run BTS! and BTS Gayo!, as well as several miniseries. BTS has almost nine million followers on V Live, and it's easy to see why. Not only can you watch a new episode of Run BTS! each Tuesday if you have a subscription, but you can watch recorded versions of all of their shows for free at any time. You can also watch vlogs where, in an intimate video blog post, each member talks about everyday life offstage like fan events, travel, or even simply cleaning the house.

Run BTS! is their variety show, where the boys face challenges and have fun together in front of the cameras for all fans to see. These boy scouts hold nothing back as they dress up like schoolgirls, face their fears, enter messy cooking challenges, come face-to-face with zombies, and, in the cutest episode ever, train puppies. The show originally aired in 2015 and continues with weekly episodes and behind-the-scenes extras on V Live.

BTS Gayo! is a musical game show where the members are the contestants each week. Challenges focus on different aspects of music, dancing, singing, and pop culture. The boys compete against each other, guessing children's songs, singing karaoke, and even

producing their own music videos. The show originally aired from 2015 to 2017, but episodes and behind-the-scenes videos can be found on the BTS V Live channel.

BTS Bon Voyage (seasons 1 & 2) is a reality show following BTS's travels. Season one aired in 2016, and features the group's ten-day tour across Northern Europe as they celebrated their third anniversary. Season two aired a year later and chronicled their nine-day Hawaiian tour.

Bokbulbok translates to fortune/misfortune. It was a five-episode game show the members played in the Big Hit HQ practice space. In each episode, a member would choose a clear plastic egg from a fish bowl that contained a game or challenge they would then need to play.

BTS Home Party occurs each year as part of the BTS Festa. The live event in Seoul is only open to certain ARMY members, but the full-length 105-minute movie can be viewed on the BTS V Live channel for free.

BTS A.R.M.Y. Rookie King *aired for eight episodes when the band was just getting started. The boys are seen cooking, bowling, goofing around, and playing games. The most popular game from the show is Endplate King, where one member was considered safe and the other six were handed cards. The word safe was written on five of the cards, and the sixth had a skull and crossbones. The unlucky skull cardholder was then handed a "punishment," like having eggs cracked on his head, having his fellow members apply makeup, smelling fermented fish, or eating spicy ramen in a sauna while wearing several layers of clothing. You can find episodes of Rookie King with English subtitles on YouTube.*

BTS Burn the Stage *airs on YouTube Red. It followed the band for three hundred days as they prepared and set off on their first world tour. The members have dedicated the show to their fans and to each other, and it celebrates the hard work, friendship, and joy of their shared journey. The show follows their setbacks and triumphs and chronicles their growth to become seasoned world-renowned artists. Burn the Stage aired its first weekly episode in March 2018.*

BTS Festa *occurs each year beginning June 1 to celebrate the anniversary of their 2013 debut. For two weeks, the group treats fans with access to free photos, songs, and videos, including behind-the-scenes access to dance practice and newly released tunes and collaborations.*

Bangtan Bomb *is a series of short videos about BTS life. Ranging from two seconds to almost ten minutes in length, the videos are random vlogs of Bangtan Sonyeondan being their everyday adorable selves. The videos are available on the Bangtan Bomb playlist on the BangtanTV YouTube channel.*

BTS AMERICAN HUSTLE LIFE TV SHOW, 2014

When the trainee Bangtan Boys started out, they worked hard every waking hour to perfect their look, their music, and their dancing, and to gel as a tight-knit group. One thing critics felt was lacking when they broke out onto the idol scene was an authentic hip-hop feel. In true leadership fashion, Bang listened to the criticism and formed a new plan: he'd send the boys to America to learn about the culture firsthand. Enter hip-hop boot camp and *American Hustle Life*.

In true Korean drama style, the boys were told they were heading to Los Angeles to record a new album. Not long after their arrival, the boys were ambushed in a staged kidnapping, where they were taken to a sketchy secret location to be "scared straight." The boys took it all in good humor and stride, and were then informed that they were actually in town to be schooled on the ins and outs of American hip-hop culture. They were introduced to mentors Dante Evans, Nate Walka, and Tony Jones, and their teachers Coolio and Warren G, and over the following two weeks, were subjected to pop quizzes, dance-offs, lessons in tough love, and above all, life-changing lessons from master artists in the field.

The boys were surprised by all they didn't know about the culture they had been embracing halfway around the world, and over the span of two weeks, they got a crash course in American music they would use to guide them from the moment they returned home.

COOLIO

CALI FRESH

BTS FEATURED ON GO!

The seventh episode of Mnet America's show Go! followed BTS on their second trip to America in 2014. The forty-four-minute show went up close and personal with the boys at Laguna Beach, visiting the Dream Factory Los Angeles live studio, and joining them onstage at KCON 2014. The show can be viewed at MnetAmerica.com.

The group loved the LA weather, beach life, seeing the sights, and living in a California mansion for the duration of their visit. The time they spent outside of lessons and doing hip-hop homework, they had fun kicking back, relaxing, and goofing around in true BTS fashion. The best part about the experience for fans was that the whole experience was caught on camera! Each week, the group released a new video chronicling their experiences. The videos captured their successes, their failures, their excitement, and their fears–the group seemed to hold nothing back in front of the camera–and fans couldn't get enough of their beagle antics!

BTS: A TRUE COMMERCIAL SUCCESS

In March 2018, BTS created an MV commercial for KB Kookmin Bank, showcasing their on-the-go app. The accompanying song: "Run," of course!

Their commercial success continued when BTS joined Team LG just a few weeks later, as LG Mobile's and LG Electronics' global ambassadors, and released commercials for Lotte Duty Free shops in four different languages.

"LDF gonna make you nice guy"
—a quote from the rap in the Lotte Duty Free commercial

Yonhap News/YNA/Newscom

Yonhap News/YNA/Newscom

Yonhap News/YNA/Newscom

Yonhap News/YNA/Newscom

Yonhap News/YNA/Newscom

Yonhap News/YNA/Newscom

Yonhap News/YNA/Newscom

BTS REACHES SUPERSTARDOM AS COCA-COLA BRAND AMBASSADORS FOR THE 2018 FIFA WORLD CUP IN RUSSIA

"We chose BTS as our models because their powerful energy on stage and passion for music matched well with the heat of the World Cup that everyone in the world enjoys, and the happiness that Coca-Cola brings in the hot summer. Starting with the Russia World Cup, Coca-Cola will be working with BTS to bring an exciting, special experience for the summer."
—Coca-Cola press release, April 29, 2018

BTS MVs

BTS music videos are visual proof that not only can these young men sing, dance, rap, produce, and compose music, they can also act! The MVs often have complex story lines that show the playful brotherhood of the band members and also tackle deep, important issues facing youth around the world.

1. June 11, 2013 "No More Dream"
2. July 16, 2013 "We Are Bulletproof Pt. 2"
3. September 10, 2013 "N.O"
4. February 11, 2014 "Boy In Luv"
5. April 4, 2014 "Just One Day"
6. August 19, 2014 "Danger"
7. October 21, 2014 "War of Hormone"
8. April 29, 2015 "I Need U"
9. June 23, 2015 "DOPE"
10. November 29, 2015 "Run"
11. April 19, 2016 "Young Forever"
12. May 1, 2016 "FIRE"
13. May 15, 2016 "Save Me"
14. October 9, 2016 "Blood Sweat & Tears"
15. February 12, 2017 "Spring Day"
16. February 19, 2017 "Not Today"
17. September 18, 2017 "DNA"

THE HYYH SERIES
Hwa Yang Yeon Hwa–The Most Beautiful Moment in Life–HYYH

The HYYH music videos tell a story of seven characters through video, music, and very little dialogue, leaving the story line wide open to interpretation. Fan theories about their meaning are everywhere, ranging from deep subjects about suicide, murder, depression, and other mental illness, to a bittersweet transition from childhood to adulthood, and offer many symbolic interpretations. While none of the theories have been confirmed or denied by BTS or Big Hit, the Bangtan Boys play into the mystery, dropping hints here and there to add fuel to the ardent flame of speculation. While the videos can be watched in any order, one prevailing theory is that this particular order makes the most sense:

- *I Need U Original Version*
- *Butterfly Prologue*
- *Run*
- *Epilogue: Young Forever*
- *Wings short films*
- *Blood Sweat & Tears*
- *Love Yourself highlight reels*
- *Spring Day*

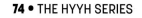

"HYYH is a four-character idiom. *Hwa yang* means the shape of flower. *Yeon hwa* means a time or moment. HYYH literally means the beautiful moment of a flower. We thought that 'HYYH' could mean youth. It means 'the most beautiful moment in life.' We think that's youth. And we hope that the time we spend together in the arena is our most beautiful moment in life."
—RM, speaking about the album, the songs, and the tour

Understanding the Music Videos
The group uses symbols throughout their music videos to convey the deeper meaning of the songs, and you don't need a 148 IQ like RM to figure them out. Most of the symbols represent the contrast of light versus darkness, youth versus experience, innocence versus wisdom, illusion versus reality, and temptation versus sacrifice. Life, as they see it, is a struggle between taking the easy way out and working hard to do the right thing and rise above the social and emotional pressures of everyday life.

Blood Sweat & Tears

A first viewing of the "Blood Sweat & Tears" MV makes most fans either thoroughly confused or very emotional. There are so many symbols and literary references, it could take a whole term paper to explain them all! Here is a breakdown of some of the symbols from the video.

1. *Jungkook flying through the air surrounded by feathers and V jumping from a high platform represents the fall that comes from having too much ambition, from the Icarus legend.*

2. *Jimin's apple represents biblical temptation.*

3. *V's arrest for vandalism represents the way authority stifles and controls artistic expression.*

4. *Jin's toast at the table represents the Last Supper, where one person sacrifices himself to save the others.*

5. *Jin kisses the statue to connect with the art. In that moment, he embraces art and the world explodes with color.*

6. *Jin's tears represent the struggle of the artist.*

Homage to Lives Lost in "Spring Day"

Demian is not the only literary reference the boys call upon. The message and MV concept of "Spring Day" is based on the award-winning fantasy short story "The Ones Who Walk Away from Omelas," by Ursula K. Le Guin. A fictional place, Omelas is supposed to be a utopian land of eternal spring, filled with equality, liberty, and innocence; however, as the story unfolds, it becomes clear that the reality is quite the opposite. "Spring Day" draws upon that feeling of loneliness and the search for happiness as BTS make their way through a series of bleak landscapes in this fictional utopia. The video is an homage to the lives lost in the Sewol ferry disaster, when a ferry sank, killing 304 people, mostly teens who were on a school trip.

The MV begins on a wintry train platform where Jungkook is completely alone. The MV is filled with symbols, from the writing on the wall that says "You'll never walk alone" where Jungkook is standing alone with the abandoned bags of unseen friends, to the flickering No Vacancy sign, to the yellow ribbon on the carousel in memory of the victims of the Sewol disaster. After a series of empty experiences that don't bring them happiness, the boys decide to leave Omelas together and seek true happiness in the outside world. The MV ends with the boys welcoming spring with meaning, light, and joy.

COLLABORATING FOR A PERFECT CHRISTMAS:
The Big Hit all-stars dropped a new holiday classic single with 2AM's Jo Kwon, Lim Jeong Hee, 8eight's Joo Hee, and BTS's RM dropping a playful rap and Jungkook singing a heartfelt solo in "Santa Claus Is Coming to Town."

BTS: BEYOND THE SONGS

Love Myself (a UNICEF Initiative)
November 1, 2017

BTS and Big Hit Entertainment joined together with Unicef to stage the campaign Love Myself as part of the larger global campaign called #ENDviolence. The program's goal is aimed at ensuring children and teens all over the world can lead safe and healthy lives without fear of violence.

To support this effort, BTS has donated proceeds from their album sales and products and urged their fans and supporters to join in and add their support as well. The money raised goes toward efforts to protect and support young victims of domestic and school violence and sexual assault, and provide educational programs to local communities.

Fans of BTS are not surprised by this outpouring of love and support for youth in need. Since their debut, the group's message of loving yourself and others is very clear. As their popularity and influence grows, these young artists see the growing opportunity to reach millions of people around the world with their message of hope, love, and nonviolence, and hope their passion for making the world a better place spreads to their ARMY of fans across the globe.

BTS Speaks Out About Depression and Mental Illness

Bang Si-hyuk, referred to as Bang PD-nim or Bang the Producer by the boys, started the band with a vision to have the group write songs that talk about things society needed to hear. The group has certainly achieved that goal, writing with openness and sincerity.

Suga and RM have both been quite outspoken about their battles with personal demons. Their songs and music videos reflect their inner struggles both as an emotional outlet for the artists, as well as a way to reach out to fans to let them know they are not alone and have an ARMY of their own supporters to help them through.

Suga's mixtape as Agust D addressed his own personal journey to becoming an idol while working through anxiety and depression. In writing the songs, he felt it was important to let his fans know that he was going through the same difficulties as they were. His songs are an invitation to find the way through it together.

> "Everyone in the world is lonely and everyone is sad, and if we know that everyone is suffering and lonely, I hope we can create an environment where we can ask for help, and say things are hard when they're hard, and say that we miss someone when we miss them."
> —Suga, *Billboard*, February 15, 2018

BTS Rally Cry

From their first single, "No More Dream," where they caution young people to follow their own dreams rather than blindly meet society's expectations, BTS has been outspoken about empowering youth to break free and think for themselves. The politically charged song "Am I Wrong" wonders aloud how people can be so blind to corruption and so immune to the sad events unfolding in the world around them. Taken together with "Spring Day," the songs are an homage to the hundreds of young lives lost on a school trip when a ferry capsized due to corruption and negligence.

Beyond their songs, the group is not shy about speaking up for what they believe in, whether it's support for protesters or support to end human suffering.

BTS: BANGTAN STYLE

Yonhap News/YNA/Newscom

Kim Nam-joon / RM

HEAD: Favorite accessory is a cap or a beanie–except in publicity photos!

BIG BRAINS: IQ of 148

EYES: Tries hard not to cry onstage

HAND: Always writing lyrics

OTHER HAND: Never leaves home without his iPhone

BODY: Loves Harajuku street style and designer Yohji Yamamoto

LEGS: Wide-legged classic '90s Levi's

FEET: Dance prodigy? Not!

"When I don't wear a cap or beanie I feel like I haven't completed my look. I have to put something on my head."

Yonhap News/YNA/Newscom

Kim Seok-jin / Jin

EYES: *Wears strong prescription glasses or contacts*

HEAD: *Worldwide Handsome*

EARS: *Ears turn red when embarrassed*

SHOULDERS: *Broad*

HAND: *Loves playing Super Mario games*

OTHER HAND: *Best cook in BTS*

FEET: *Avid snowboarder*

Jin got his nickname "car door guy" when he was caught on camera looking handsome while exiting a vehicle. The internet blew up with fans wanting to identify this mystery man.

Min Yoon-gi / Suga

BODY: Always wearing jewelry

HEAD: Likes quiet places

BODY: Sleeps whenever, wherever

HAND: Likes reading comics and the Ikea catalog

OTHER HAND: Plays basketball

FEET: Collects Michael Jordan shoes

Although Suga is a crackerjack performer and idol, when he's offstage, he prefers quiet places to large crowds.

Yonhap News/YNA/Newscom

Jung Ho-seok / J-Hope

HEAD: *Good problem-solver*

MOUTH: *Loves to eat*

CHEEKS: *Blushes when he brags*

BODY: *Doesn't like to exercise or work out*

LEGS: *Favorite pants and jeans style is clean-cut, not baggy*

HAND: *Likes to check in with BTS ARMY at the fancafe*

J-Hope's bandmates compare him to the character Doraemon, a Japanese manga robot cat who has a solution to every problem.

Park Ji-min / Jimin

TOP OF HEAD: Shortest BTS member

HEAD: Likes bandannas and snapback caps

EYES: Wears eyeliner when rehearsing

FACE: Doesn't love his puffy cheeks

ABS: Proud of his rock-hard abs

FEET: Dances anytime, anywhere

Jimin is as humble as he is talented, and plays down his own accomplishments while complimenting others.

Yonhap News/YNA/Newscom

Kim Tae-hyung / V

FACE: Nicknamed Blank Tae for his blank expression

EYES: Has an eye for photography

HAIR: Accidentally cut his own hair while shooting "Danger" MV

HAND: Bites his nails

OTHER HAND: Can climb a tree (but can't get down)

FEET: Doesn't like wearing shoes

V is scared of ghosts.

Jeon Jeong-guk / Jungkook

FACE: Doesn't usually express his feelings

MOUTH: Hates bland food

BODY: Most athletic

HAND: Most artistic

OTHER HAND: Most competitive BTS member

FEET: Loves shoes–especially his Timberland boots

Jungkook sniffles all the time because he suffers from bad allergies.

K-POP TERMS

4D: *Korean slang used to describe someone who has a weird or unique personality. It's more of a compliment than an insult. This can also be used for someone who has a strong personality and tends to think outside the box and be creative (usually in a weird sort of way). Fans say V's personality is 4D.*

AEGYO: *A display of cuteness, like winking, forming a hand heart, or blowing a kiss. BTS members are always showing love to their fans with their adorable aegyo moves, making them the most meme-able and gif-able band around.*

ALL-KILL: *Hitting number one on all eight Korean music charts: Melon, Mnet, Bugs, Olleh, Soribada, Genie, Naver, and Monkey3 charts.*

BAGEL: *A baby face with a glamorous, sexy body, like Park Ji-min!*

BEAGLE: *An idol who is loud, boisterous, and can't sit still for even a moment. Beagles are always being noisy, playing around, and causing mischief. When they get too annoying, a beagle can quickly be called kkab instead.*

BIAS: *Your absolute favorite celebrity whom you support no matter what. Not every BTS fan has a bias . . . most fans find it hard to choose.*

CHOCOLATE ABS: *Abs that are so strongly defined, their lines resemble the blocks on a chocolate bar.*

COMEBACK: *The first release of a new title track, album, or single.*

DAEBAK: *Big success.*

DONGSAENG: *Friend who is younger than you. It's like calling someone your "little buddy."*

FAN CHANT: *A chant created to go along with the melody of a specific song. Sometimes they are chanted in response to specific words in the song, like in "DNA." Other times fans chant the names of the members in order: Kim Nam-joon! Kim Seok-jin! Min Yoon-gi! Jung Ho-seok! Park Ji-min! Kim Tae-hyung! Jeon Jeong-guk! BTS!*

HALLYU: *"Korean wave." Fandom for all things Korean, including food, TV, language, and of course, K-pop.*

HYUNG: *"Older brother." (All of the older members are hyung to Jung-kook, the maknae of the group.) If you are a gal, you call older gals unni and older guys oppa. If you are a guy, you call older guys hyung and older gals noona. Unni and noona can be translated to older sister. Oppa and hyung can be translated to older brother.*

KKAB: *A "beagle" whose cute antics go over-the-top and become annoying instead.*

JJANG: *The best! If you like something, give it two thumbs-up and say "Jjang!"*

MAKNAE: *Youngest in a group. (Jungkook is the maknae of BTS.)*

MANHWA: *The Korean term for comics. It includes comic books, manga, animation, and webtoons. Hip Hop Monster (or Hipmon) and We On are official BTS webtoons.*

MUKBANG: *A video of a Korean idol enjoying large quantities of food on camera while talking to the audience. Eat Jin is a very popular mukbang series available on YouTube.*

OPPA: *Technically translated as "older brother," oppa is usually a term girls use when they're talking to or about their crush.*

OTP: One true pairing, one true ship, or simply shipping is a big part of K-pop culture. Fans love to fantasize about pairing two favorite idols with each other, often regardless of gender. The BTS fandom is filled with ideas on which BTS members to ship with each other and with K-pop stars. Often shipping comes with a combined name, like pairing Jungkook and Suga would become SugaKookie!

SASAENG: Obsessive fans who do crazy things to get close to their idols. No matter how much you love BTS, don't be a sasaeng–join the ARMY instead!

SATOORI: Dialect or accent. The Korean language has two main satooris: Daegu and Busan. Jimin sometimes feels embarrassed by his Busan satoori, while V is proud of his Daegu. In Seoul, locals find country accents to be endearing!

SELCA: A combination of the words "self" and "camera," it means the same as "selfie" in Korean. The Bangtan Boys are masters at the selca, always posting their antics online for fans–and sometimes with fans, too.

SOOMPI AWARDS: *Fan-driven awards honoring the best of the best in Korean television and music. Winners are determined based on web votes and Soompi Music Chart scores, and reflect an artist's or group's popularity worldwide.*

SSANTI: *A silly dance idols perform for fans. All BTS members have killer moves, but they have been known to shake their booties ssanti-style when they're goofing around behind the scenes.*

TRAINEE: *Before K-pop stars make their big debut, they go through months of rigorous training that involves strict diet and exercise routines and long hours of hard work. When a trainee's work is complete, they become an idol.*

TSUNDERE: *The word is a combination of Japanese word tsun, which refers to someone who acts blunt, and dere, someone who is affectionate. So the word describes someone who acts cold at first but slowly warms up to others. Suga is considered by some fans to be tsundere.*

VISUAL: *The best-looking member of the group. This is not always the same as the "face of the group," which is often the most popular member. The role of visual in BTS is filled by Jin, self-described "worldwide handsome."*

Fans Ask: Will Bangtan Boys still be "Bangtan Boys" 20 years later? "Of course. It's hard to say until it's that time, but there could be a chance we change names. I've thought of a lot. 'Bangtan Middle-Aged Group,' 'BTS,' 'Bangtan Man,' etc. But what's important isn't the name. The most important thing is wanting to become a group that is still together in twenty years." —RM in group interview with *AJ x The Star*

BTS AND THE
OTHER ARMY

South Korean law requires all men between the ages of eighteen and thirty-five to serve in the military for twenty-one months. While management and production companies used to be able to postpone or choose when their members serve, a new law states that idols can no longer get special treatment and must come when they're called. People who follow Hallyu (the Korean pop culture wave) see this all the time when their favorite movie and TV stars disappear from the scene for a while. Production companies often promote the comeback of the most popular bias with a lot of fanfare.

When will Bangtan Sonyeondan be called up? How will it affect the music, the fans, and the performances? Only time will tell.